An Ark

A Play for Mixed Reality

An Ark
A Play for Mixed Reality

Simon Stephens

methuen | drama
LONDON • NEW YORK • OXFORD • NEW DELHI • SYDNEY

METHUEN DRAMA

Bloomsbury Publishing Plc, 50 Bedford Square, London, WC1B 3DP, UK
Bloomsbury Publishing Inc, 1359 Broadway, New York, NY 10018, USA
Bloomsbury Publishing Ireland, 29 Earlsfort Terrace, Dublin 2,
D02 AY28, Ireland

BLOOMSBURY, METHUEN DRAMA and the Methuen
Drama logo are trademarks of Bloomsbury Publishing Plc.

First published in Great Britain 2026

Copyright © Simon Stephens, 2026

Simon Stephens has asserted his right under the Copyright, Designs
and Patents Act, 1988, to be identified as author of this work.

Cover photography: Ian McKellen, Golda Rosheuvel,
Arinzé Kene and Rosie Sheehy © Rachel Louise Brown

All rights reserved. No part of this publication may be: i) reproduced or
transmitted in any form, electronic or mechanical, including photocopying,
recording or by means of any information storage or retrieval system without
prior permission in writing from the publishers; or ii) used or reproduced in
any way for the training, development or operation of artificial intelligence (AI)
technologies, including generative AI technologies. The rights holders
expressly reserve this publication from the text and data mining exception as
per Article 4(3) of the Digital Single Market Directive (EU) 2019/790.

Bloomsbury Publishing Plc does not have any control over, or responsibility
for, any third-party websites referred to or in this book. All internet addresses
given in this book were correct at the time of going to press. The author and
publisher regret any inconvenience caused if addresses have changed or sites
have ceased to exist, but can accept no responsibility for any such changes.

No rights in incidental music or songs contained in the work are hereby
granted and performance rights for any performance/presentation
whatsoever must be obtained from the respective copyright owners.

All rights whatsoever in this play are strictly reserved and application
for performance etc. should be made before rehearsals to Casarotto Ramsay
& Associates Ltd., 3rd Floor, 7 Savoy Court, Strand, London, WC2R 0EX.

No performance may be given unless a licence has been obtained.

A catalogue record for this book is available from the British Library.

Library of Congress Control Number: 2025951390

ISBN: PB: 978-1-3506-3243-1
ePDF: 978-1-3506-3246-2
eBook: 978-1-3506-3245-5

Series: Modern Plays

Typeset by Mark Heslington Ltd, Scarborough, North Yorkshire
Printed and bound in the United States of America

For product safety related questions contact
productsafety@bloomsbury.com.

To find out more about our authors and books visit
www.bloomsbury.com and sign up for our newsletters.

An Ark originally opened at The Shed in New York City on 9 January 2026. Presented by The Shed and Tin Drum, with the following cast and creative team.

A **Ian McKellen**
B **Golda Rosheuvel**
C **Arinzé Kene**
D **Rosie Sheehy**

Writer	Simon Stephens
Director	Sarah Frankcom
Produced and Commissioned by	Todd Eckert
Set and Wardrobe Design	Rosanna Vize
Production Company	Tin Drum
Sound Design and Composition	Ben and Max Ringham
Lighting Design	Seth Reiser
Casting	Shaheen Baig
Volumetric Capture	4D Views, Grenoble, France

An Ark

A Play for Mixed Reality

A large room with space for 50 audience members.

Simple chairs.

Each audience member sits in a space made with four performers.

A, **B**, **C** *and* **D**

The room starts in house lights so that all the audience members can see one another.

It falls imperceptibly slowly but gets to the point that all the audience members can see is the performers.

A   Don't panic.

B   Don't panic.

A   Don't be scared.

C   This must feel strange to you.

D   It felt strange to me – I still remember it now, like it was –

A   You must have known this was going to happen.

B   We all know this moment is going to happen.

C   Most people choose to pretend that it won't.

A   When this is all over, you'll go through the doorway at the end of the room. On the other side of the doorway things will have changed forever.

B   You'll want to tell people about the things that have happened to you in here.

A   And the things that happened to you.

C   All the things that have ever happened to you.

B   They matter.

D   Do they?

B   They do.

4 An Ark

A You're born in a town on the coast.

C You're born in the suburbs of a major city.

B You're born in the rural heartlands of your country surrounded by farms for as far as the eye can see.

D You're born in a desert. An actual desert.

B It's a huge shock.

D It's just normal.

A It's astonishing.

D It is the most normal thing in the world. There is nothing astonishing about it at all.

A The chances of birth on the one planet we know that can accommodate life.

D I mean –

A The mathematical possibility that out of the millions and millions and millions of sperm there is one that fertilises its egg and leads –

B To you.

A Is so slight!

C And yet here you are.

A Chromosomes turned into flesh and eyes and taste and smell and incredible sound and the magic of the trillion electrodes triggered by a brain that still keeps growing.

B For years.

C For about seven years I think.

A pause.

D There is part of you that still remembers the shock.

B The first blast of air in an open lung.

D She is covered in blood.

A Thick and warm and then the first rush into the long and desperate cold and the blanket wrapped warm around you and this is everything.

D You're so scared.

A The smell of your mother.

D She's scared too. All women get scared, you know?

A The feeling of her skin on your skin or the sounds that you have somehow heard through the thick warm walls of her. The possibility of colour. The songs that your father sings.

C You have heard these songs before.

A On the day you are born there is a rainbow in the sky to the west of the hospital.

C Your mother's brother tells you when you are five years old.

A The feeling of being held as high as your father can hold you and thrown into a blue sky.

C One! Two! Three!

D Wheee!

B A series of strange houses you can't remember with people you've not met before, but they are all friendly to you. And then you find one and you're told you can stay.

D A warm paddling pool in the afternoon. Wet cold feet. Ice cream.

C And what's weird is that these other people, the other people in this room, they remember all that too.

D The smell of finger paints.

B The sense that there are things you can't control.

A The bubble of blood on your knee as you fall on hard concrete.

D And numbers. And how they add up.

A And how they divide. And how they multiply.

B The size of the universe as you try to remember the list of the planets.

A Mercury. Venus. Earth. Mars. Jupiter. Saturn. Uranus.

C Ha.

A Neptune.

B These strange thoughts you think no human has had before.

D You hold hands when you line up to go to the lunch room.

B Nobody else has a family like the one you live with.

D Partners, hold hands please!

C Your hand has grown now. Look at it. It has been broken and kissed and bruised and cherished. It has smacked and masturbated. It feels like it must be a different hand to the hand you had then but it's not. It's the same. Can you see?

A You're seven years old.

B You go on a weekend away with your new parents to a cottage by the coast and it is here where for the first time in your life you swim in the sea.

A The feeling and the smell of grass cut fresh on a spring morning. Your whole life you will have this sense that nobody has smelled grass cut like this.

C You lie on your back and stare at the sky. The white vapour trails of the planes are like secret codes. A promise written just for you. There are some things only you can understand.

B This is the life you will have.

D You're seven and a half.

A The feeling of the woollen sweater that you wear to school.

C You nearly understand some grown-up words now.

A In these words, the world reveals itself to you.

D You are amazed how easy it is to make another child cry. Actually cry as they start to realise that the stories you're telling each other about them are very different from the stories they're telling themselves.

B 'I thought you liked me. Why are you being so horrible to me?'

C The feeling of air filling your lungs as the school gathers to watch each other play sports. You know some of them are paying particular attention to you.

A Cherry blossom. Chocolate milk. Night terrors.

B The sound of your new mother's voice as she tells you to be careful.

D There are, to be fair, some things you need to be careful of.

A The way your heart stops when you see your best friend.

B You're 8 years old.

C If you look closely into the earth in the field near your house you can see that there is a world in there. The insects in the soil.

D Even at that age you understand that your life will be defined by your perspective on it.

A You can imagine the microbes in the space between each blade of grass.

B You're suddenly worried that they will be furious with you for being out so late.

D 'Look at that dirt on your clothes.'

C But the air is so crisp, and that crispness means that after a while you're not worried anymore about the way she looks at you.

D At school you work hard but you never really feel like you belong.

C You're nine years old. Your father takes you to the swimming pool. You let the water get in your eyes. It doesn't frighten you at all.

B You are scared of the sounds of your house moving in the night, though.

C You sing your favourite television programme's theme tune to yourself to take the sounds away.

A Your first days of school holiday.

D How long it takes you to get bored.

A If I could tell you all the things you have ever known have existed in the dance between the neurones in your mind, would you believe me?

B You come alive to the feeling of cycling by the side of the water.

C You come alive to the feeling of silk on skin.

D You wonder why boys aren't allowed to enjoy soft things.

B You watch your parents dancing. You wonder if one day you will dance with somebody like that too.

A The feeling when your father puts you on his shoulders and walks you home because it's late now.

C The city at night.

D You come alive to the old eyes of your grandmother smiling. And the way she sang and sang.

C Did you ever smile like she still smiles in your mind?

B Here. Can I touch you?

A Don't flinch. Don't move. Don't panic.

B I'm real you know. I'm as real as anything.

B *moves to nearly touch the audience. The others watch.*

C You're fourteen. You can run 100 metres in 12 seconds.

D All the rage you felt. Teenage and brutal and full of a sense of that injustice. And the sense that you wanted to tear all this down. Cut the paper. Chop an axe into a broken tree. Scream to the sky. Burn the wind.

A Stand frozen in the raging summer sun.

D You can't stand it when he moves away from you. You want to touch him all the time. You want to lean against him. His smooth skin and the light, tight muscles of his arms. You feel the body shock of orgasm for the first time.

B In time it becomes clear to you that he's only doing it to see what would happen if he did. You come to learn a little in future years about nuance and self-doubt and shame but this feels unforgivable.

D He breaks your heart.

C You want to set yourself on fire.

B It really hurts. You feel humiliated.

A But, of course, in time the blood will flow again.

B You never stop being excited by the wind coming off the sea.

D Or the sun on the back of your neck.

C You score twice in the regional youth cup final when you're seventeen. Somebody says a scout has come to watch you play. He tells your dad that your speed is unlike anything he's seen in seven years. You notice the three girls who have come to the front of the stand by the wing you're playing and who change sides at half time so they can follow you round the pitch. Your second goal gets so many hits on TikTok. People lose their shit. So it takes you quite some time to get over the surprise when your youth contract expires and the promised interest from other clubs doesn't materialise.

B Your best friend is studying French. She spends the third year of her degree in a school in Paris. You think about going to stay with her for a term.

D The pain of disappointment is unlike anything you've ever known.

C You struggle with coaching for a couple of years and spend four more trying to set up an agency to help young professional players navigate the property market.

B You lie in bed curled into a ball. You can't move. She wraps herself around you and strokes your hair. Your hair is the only part of you that doesn't hurt.

D Two years later you hear a story about the big brother of the boy from your school.

C He was older than a lot of you, but everybody thought of him as their friend.

B Well. Not a friend.

C But everybody knew him.

D The day you all went to the festival.

A The kind of place where you felt neither excited nor comfortable.

C You told the girl you met there that you were good to drive.

B Some boys carry a sense of their own immortality.

D She ended up with the gear shift sticking into the side of her kidney.

C You were trapped in your seat and so you were able to watch her eyes close and feel your fear fade before you smelled gas. You tried to scream but there was blood in your throat caught like a bubble.

A Time is a field and whichever way you look it goes on to the horizon.

C You understood in that moment that the future would see a hundred thousand more boys like you on summer days like this one.

D Was that something that you did? Did you do that too?

C *doesn't answer.*

D Are you done now?

C No. I'm not done. It's too soon.

D Are you allowed to carry on? Is he allowed to even be here if he's done something like that?

A brief pause.

A It's a decision he needs to make for himself.

C *leaves.*

A Thank you.

B You still think about her smile sometimes.

A You wonder for the first time what it really feels like to die.

D You wonder for the first time about the fragility of your own mind.

B You wonder if other people think the thoughts you think.

D They don't.

B You start to realise that you've lost something, and you wonder if it might be immense.

A But sometimes there are moments when you follow an idea to its logical conclusion and it feels more electrifying than can possibly make sense.

B You have never imagined that the colour of a dress could stop your heart.

D You read books that make you feel less alone suddenly.

B One summer, you head down to the waterfall. You've never known water so powerful. The way the sun reflects on her shining hair. If you could bottle a day. You know now what it is to be kissed.

A You find yourself aware of the way your body looks. Your body doesn't look like other boys'.

D Your body doesn't look like other girls'.

A You find yourself focusing on the way thought makes you happy.

D And when you're not even twenty you go the drug store for the test and you stare at it for hours in the toilets at college.

And months later. Your baby is very beautiful. The sight of her in pain is like a kind of madness. At one point you're almost laughing. And then – I can't do this next bit. I'm sorry.

Some time.

B You find yourself, at twenty-three, with money of your own for the first time.

A You travel abroad for the first time without your parents.

B You love it.

A You don't.

B You feel so free.

A You know yourself to be a very different person to your parents.

B You know yourself to feel your parents in a place hidden in your bones.

A It seems the older you get the more things you understand to be unsettling.

B The more things you understand to be exciting. Not unsettling. Exciting.

A Don't panic.

B They're not panicking.

D They are. You can see it in the way their pupils open.

B That's just the light in this room.

D Come here. Have a look at this on the side of the neck.

B It's a pulse. It just means they're alive.

A You walk across a field in the middle of an August night. The soil dry and hard underfoot and the sense of being on the curve of a moon rock and the sense of the scale of a year makes you, quite unexpectedly, want to lie on the ground with astonishment.

B The edge of the glacier on the distant mountain in the moonlight casts a kind of light over the valley.

A You find your fingers unbuttoning the buttons of a shirt.

B Other fingers touch your belly, and you start to shake.

D You spend a great deal of your life in despair at how stupid and pointless people are. Imagine your surprise at twenty-five after everything that's happened, when you find yourself falling in love. In a hotel room overlooking the river.

B This person offers to give their life to you and asks if you'll do the same.

D It feels like a wave.

A Their hair smells like lemongrass.

B Their eyes look so deeply into yours it's like they are examining your skeleton. You feel for the briefest time like you're flying.

D You can't stop laughing.

A You can't stop crying.

D You dance all night.

B Kiss me. Kiss me again. Not like that. Like that.

D Touch me. Touch me there.

A In this universe it is impossible to create energy. It is impossible to waste energy. All you can do is pass it on.

B All the sadness is held in her tremble.

D Afterwards the two of you fold into one another. Your feet are bare on the hotel floor. The river turns through the city in the nighttime.

B You didn't know that it was possible for two people to blur the edges like this.

A Don't tell anybody. If people found out, if anybody found out, if the other people in this room found out that you two had bled into one another like this. Your atoms bouncing into one another and breaking the edges of each other.

B You love her so much that your heart literally skips the moment she walks into your room.

A The passion with which she speaks and the utter certainty of her sadness almost confuses you.

B The two of you dance together.

D You watch him sleep and you've never seen anything like it in your life. You wonder what kind of a father he would have made.

B She remembers every word you have ever said to her.

A Her memory is what most startles you.

B You kneel before her.

A She says –

B Yes.

D He's crying.

B You don't tell her not to cry. Why do people tell each other not to cry? If we have anything of any value, it's the way we can cry.

D There are things you could explain to him.

A You're too scared. And so. In time.

A brief pause. They all hold the audience's gaze.

B And then you're thirty-one. You begin to become aware of the overwhelming age of trees. You almost resent them for the things they've seen.

D You take to buying more expensive shoes and cut your hair short.

B You and you wife agree to spend less time looking at your phones and more time reading books.

A Your eyesight starts to weaken.

D The edges of things start to blur.

A You know that sense –

D That fear –

B That love –

C *comes back. They notice him.*

C If you could come back. And not have done the things you've done. And live.

D You can't come back. Can he come back?

*The others look at **C** briefly.*

C Please.

A We keep going. We go on.

C *sits back down with the group.*

B You're forty years old. You spend so long wondering whether or not you should have a baby that you decide that if you really wanted one then you wouldn't be so indecisive. You realise one day in the dairy aisle of your local supermarket that yours is a body that will now never know what it's like to give birth.

D You've worked in the same job for ten years and when somebody tells you that you feel a bit confused.

B That can't be right. How did that happen?

A Remind me what job this is exactly?

D You have absolutely no memory of what the job is or why you have stayed working there for ten years.

B But you have.

D You drink five litres of water a day. For a while.

B You feel like you should carry a bucket or something. Measure it out.

D You do these things to try to convince yourself that you're not going to die. That it won't get you in the end.

C That you haven't made a mistake.

B You meet her at a seminar in a hotel in Buenos Aires. You've never seen anybody laugh like that. You've never seen anybody look at you like that before. She knew then that you would think about her for the rest of your life. To have that chance and know it was taken away because you are married.

A And you were scared.

C And you loved your wife. Never let it be said that you didn't love your wife. Because you did.

B But to be looked at in that way. To hold somebody like that.

D Years later. Years after you never saw her again, she would still be with you. Just there on the edges of your vision and in some bruised quiet place in the corner of your heart.

A At fifty-two you realise you have become surprisingly enthusiastic about gardening.

D Nobody expected that.

C I did.

D You didn't.

C Look at the way they're sitting.

A You find yourself, one October, suddenly moved by the idea of nutrients in the soil and the possibility to grow colour. Where there was no colour you made colour grow for the first time from the moist black dirt of the ground.

B The lines on the skin around your face begin to take you by surprise and you can't really figure out if the things you thought happened to you ever actually happened to you or if they were just an edge of a kind of dream.

D You work for a while as a manager of a seafood restaurant and become fascinated by the way your customers look at you when they pay their bill.

C You're haunted by the sound of schoolkids playing football in the street.

B The warning of a garbage truck reversing outside your window.

A They let you visit your father in the hospice at the edge of the village and you can't take your eyes off him.

B If I could hold hands with you and take all the fear away I would.

A The way he breathes. He tells you to stop talking. He tells you your hands are soft. He tells you to touch him. You tell him that none of this disappears. This stays. The things he has done will outlive him.

D He looks at you, his eyes a sad shadow of non-recognition. 'I don't know who you are.'

A You are a middle-aged man with a love of hill walking.

B You are a woman in her late fifties wondering who her mother was and afraid of the things she can feel in her body.

C You take to swimming in the night.

A In the nighttime your skin in water looks like folds and creases.

D Nobody replies to your emails anymore.

A There are baffling nights of exultation and certainty.

B At work people kind of stop noticing you. And then it's not just at work. It feels like it's everywhere. And then they are just confused that you are somehow still in the room.

D Are you somehow still in the room?

C You're fifty-eight. You're old newspapers. A yellow silk shirt. Battered blue jeans. Green tea and mineral water.

A You get on first name terms with your pharmacist.

C You start going to places you didn't even know were possible to go to.

B You value financial stability and begin thinking differently about God.

A You start to make noises when you stand up. There are aches and stretches and sounds in your back and your lumber and your hips.

C The idea that there are insects you didn't realise even existed only inches away from the surface of the Earth still amazes you.

B You and your wife go for walks every evening.

C You feel a sense of awe sometimes without knowing why.

B Do you know why?

A I think they are becoming aware of the smallness of a planet they have always thought to be large. And the frankly unimaginable space they come to understand exists between planets throughout the solar system.

C As you get older you struggle to tell the difference between what's true and what isn't anymore. The difference between something you imagined and something that happened to you.

A If you could have you would have moved to the countryside.

D Headed to the mountains.

B Woken up at 6 just to see the dawn rise over the edge.

D Built a shed to work in.

C Dug the foundations yourself.

A Cut the edge of your spade into the cold earth.

D The sound of metal on cold ground takes you back to grave diggers.

A As a consequence of the increasing popularity of cremation for economic and ecological reasons you only ever saw one actual graveside.

B The teenage child of your friend who died at fifteen one Christmas Eve.

A The cold blue skies of winter.

B The Earth is warming. It can't take much more of this.

D You'll die before the Earth does. Don't worry about that.

C Do you sometimes like to imagine the end of the world?

D Is it easier to imagine that than to think about how the world will continue long after you've died?

A Your skin got old.

B You're starting to find that beautiful.

A You take off your shoes and socks and put your foot, its old skin spotted, in the moving water.

B You're sixty-seven. It's November.

A There is ice on the edges of the water.

D Can you reach for my hand? Can you feel it?

B Don't.

D What you need to know is that if you come with me all the grief and all the shame will go away. All the fear will go away too. And all the regret. And the knowledge of how much pain she was in as you watched her and weren't able to help her. Hold my hand and come to the edge of the lake.

B You mustn't.

D Take off your shoes and socks. It will make it easier.

B No.

D Fold your clothes by the shore. Leave your phone. The tide can take you.

B No.

D You have been alive long enough now. The town's closed down. The cars don't pass here at this time of year. You feel the winter air and the water lapping around your ankles. You see the fish shy away from you. In the end all this will pass to thin air and sand. You look at the way the moon shines on the surface. The water moves when you walk into it. Cut the surface and plunge.

A pause. They look at the audience member.

It's the strangest thing to see.

To know what is going to happen to you.

The water fills your lungs.

B   And consciousness fills your mind.

A   And you come back. Lie on the cold stones on the beach, breathing hard.

C   You can't make the sound of a word. You lose all sense of the shape and meaning of words.

B   It's like you remember the sounds that you made in the first breath. You remember the feeling of opening up your lungs.

A   There is no time anymore for thoughts like these.

C   Every year you get more curious about the way time seems to move forward.

A   A whole season spent staring out of the fucking window.

They notice **A** *swearing.*

C   New Year stops being an exciting time and starts being an uncertain one.

B   Each year starts to feel like a weird re-enactment of the last.

C   Maybe the point is that wishing people happy new year kind of kindles happiness in and of itself.

A   It might be worth paying attention to that.

B   And that new ache.

D   That's the second time you felt that ache.

C   And you want to look up the symptoms on the Internet, but you're scared to.

A One afternoon, four days after your birthday, you start coughing after you park your car in the garage, and you look down into your handkerchief and you realise that it's not blood you've coughed up.

D It's something thick and black.

A You realise after a while that, well, it's not that you don't feel pain. You do.

C Your back hurts.

A All the time.

B Your bones are crumbling. You're shrinking, which puts pressure on the nerve endings in your spinal column.

D It's not that the pain doesn't bother you anymore.

A Nothing bothers you anymore.

D The sharp stabs in your spine.

C Toothache.

B The sting where your skin has opened because you've been scratching your eczema.

A But you feel good things.

C The sweet taste of Coca-Cola. The plunge in your heart of a love story. The view of the horizon in the sky as the sun falls.

B More than any of those things it's when you come into contact with water.

A When you stand under a cold shower.

B When you put an ice cube on your tongue.

C You have started to watch the people you grow up with die.

D You spend spring mornings in overly warm hospital rooms trying secretly to speed the whole process up.

B   And then –

C   Of course.

A   After you get your diagnosis, the second you leave the doctor you are overwhelmed by the sense of how beautiful it is to have existed at all and known the wonder of consciousness.

B   You're eighty years old.

C   You're a woollen dress. You're black boots.

A   And your eyes *do* sparkle with a life spent savouring each moment.

C   Like your grandmother's did. I thought they would.

B   The view over a lake in April as it stretches on for miles.

D   Black water.

A   The curious sense that things have shrunk here.

B   The sense of something awful being about to happen.

C   Don't look behind you.

D   Look behind you.

B   It's okay.

A   If this is really how things end – Is this really how things end?

D   This is how things end.

A slight pause.

A   You find yourself surprised by how funny you find most people under the age of seven now.

B   You have strong feelings about your funeral arrangements even though if there was one event you were guaranteed not to be able to attend it is that one.

A I would have thought if there was one event you were guaranteed to be able to attend –

D No laughing. No crying. Keep your eyes focused on the horizon.

A You die in the oncology wing of a major hospital. For as long as you can remain conscious you are fascinated by the mathematics of the measurements they take and the dosages they prescribe. Your nephew is with you. He is stunned by the light in the room and the slowness of your breathing and the way your skin seems as thin as paper. He has to get back to work. He's startled by the speed and efficiency with which they come to clean your body and take you out of the ward.

C You never tell anybody that you piss your pants at the moment you die and all of the jokes you ever heard come rushing to your mind at once as you lie in the car trying to breathe.

B You're looking to see if the robin has come to the birdfeed in your back garden on a sunny Wednesday afternoon when you are startled by a piercing pain in the back of your skull. You fall down dead five minutes later.

D You die in the deep lake three miles from the reservoir near your house. The rain is lashing against the surface of the water but you can't hear it anymore.

B It's the warmth that will surprise you.

C It's not a frightening heat. It will make you feel sleepy but in a way that you'll find kind of nice. Your vision blurs. You reach for your glasses but then you remember that you were kind of wearing them and ever so slowly the light starts to fade.

A You fade and disappear.

A moment.

B After you die you start to realise that people have managed to carry on their lives perfectly well without you.

C When you die nobody will know what to do with your clothes.

B In a few days people are able to start joking about you.

A Certain smells will bring your memory back to them like a rush.

D They will stop renewing your Internet account so that your e-mail account will fall out of use other than in pretty basic phishing scams.

A And if you could go back the thing that you would most want to do is breathe.

C Which is odd because it was something you never really noticed when you were alive.

B How amazing a breath is.

C You will also regret not taking more naps.

A The remarkable thing is that these people in this room will gather around your bedside after you die. They will be rather surprised to see one another again.

B Some of the people will bring flowers.

C Some will be surprisingly moved by the death of somebody they never really met.

B Some of them will wonder if you have left them anything, which is a bit weird.

D Some of them are acting out of a weird prurience.

A But they will be there.

B There will be a rainbow over the river in your hometown.

A There was a rainbow on the day you were born. Your uncle told you that when you were small.

B You only remember it now at this precise second.

A Before you were born the world turned in wild storms for millions of years. When the rains stopped an electrochemical impulse that nobody has ever understood put energy into a molecule in the sea. And the molecule grew and swam and climbed from the sea and onto the ground and moved to the plains and the mountains and the desert. And learned how to talk and how to kill and the sense of astonishment at the strange way in which we know we lose things. We do. We lose everything. At the last moment everything you ever had you will lose. But despite knowing this, knowing all this, you still have somehow largely managed to live with kindness and curiosity and somehow managed to live with love.

B You need to know that humans survive after you die.

A Engineers still have the capacity to invent and they turn this capacity to all manner of things. Not just habitation and temperature control but food supply and water distillation and distribution of the arts and sport.

B And people still go for walks.

C Long old walks on spring days under red skies.

D Night still falls.

A And in the very last moments, we walk to the edge of an extraordinary crevice and all the humans who have ever lived stand at the edge of this crevice looking down into the darkness below.

D And one by one, all of us, we step out into the darkness.

B Some of us try to stop ourselves from falling.

C Some of us hold our breath as though we're jumping into water.

A Some of us know what is happening and we leap.

B Some of us turn back and try to hold eye contact with the ones we leave behind.

C We can't.

A We still try.

D We fall too quickly.

A We still try.

B Wait.

D Don't go.

A I'm turning into something I no longer understand.

A disappears.

D Is that it?

B Not yet.

C Has he gone now?

B I think so.

D Are we done?

B No. Look. They're still sitting here.

D Is that rain?

C I think it started to rain.

Have you noticed how strange everybody else in this room seems?

B Have you wondered what would happen if you took that man's hand, that man there and you held onto it.

C Or what if you suddenly inhabited a memory of a place you've never been to?

B Or a person. That woman, for example, she's not sure if the smell of her mother is really the smell of *her* mother or if, in some way, she has her mother confused with yours.

C Everything you've ever done you realise that people in this room remember doing that now.

B Everything you have ever known, they know.

C The places you've been.

B The love that you've known.

D Where are we meant to go?

B Come with me.

C Out of the door at the end of the room.

D What are we going to do?

B We keep going. We go on.

DRAMA ONLINE

Discover. Read. Listen. Watch.

A NEW WAY TO ENGAGE WITH PLAYS

This award-winning digital library features over 3,000 playtexts, 400 audio plays, 300 hours of video and 360 scholarly books.

Playtexts published by Methuen Drama, The Arden Shakespeare, Faber & Faber, Playwrights Canada Press, Aurora Metro Books and Nick Hern Books.

Audio Plays from L.A. Theatre Works featuring classic and modern works from the oeuvres of leading American playwrights.

Video collections including films of live performances from the RSC, The Globe and The National Theatre, as well as acting masterclasses and BBC feature films and documentaries.

FIND OUT MORE:
www.dramaonlinelibrary.com • @dramaonlinelib

Methuen Drama World Classics
include

Jean Anouilh (two volumes)
Brendan Behan
Aphra Behn
Bertolt Brecht (eight volumes)
Büchner
Bulgakov
Calderón
Čapek
Anton Chekhov
Noël Coward (eight volumes)
Feydeau (two volumes)
Eduardo De Filippo
Max Frisch
John Galsworthy
Gogol
Gorky (two volumes)
Harley Granville Barker
(two volumes)
Victor Hugo
Henrik Ibsen (six volumes)
Jarry
Lorca (three volumes)
Marivaux
Mustapha Matura
David Mercer (two volumes)
Arthur Miller (six volumes)
Molière
Musset
Peter Nichols (two volumes)
Joe Orton
A. W. Pinero
Luigi Pirandello
Terence Rattigan
(two volumes)
W. Somerset Maugham
(two volumes)
August Strindberg
(three volumes)
J. M. Synge
Ramón del Valle-Inclán
Frank Wedekind
Oscar Wilde

Methuen Drama Modern Plays

include

Bola Agbaje
Ayad Akhtar
Edward Albee
Jean Anouilh
John Arden
Peter Barnes
Clare Barron
Sebastian Barry
Alistair Beaton
Brendan Behan
Edward Bond
William Boyd
Bertolt Brecht
Howard Brenton
Amelia Bullmore
Anthony Burgess
Leo Butler
Jim Cartwright
Lolita Chakrabarti
Caryl Churchill
Lucinda Coxon
Tim Crouch
Shelagh Delaney
Ishy Din
Claire Dowie
David Edgar
David Eldridge
Dario Fo
Michael Frayn
John Godber
James Graham
David Greig
John Guare
Lauren Gunderson
Peter Handke
David Harrower
Jonathan Harvey
Robert Holman
David Ireland
Sarah Kane

Barrie Keeffe
Jasmine Lee-Jones
Anders Lustgarten
Duncan Macmillan
David Mamet
Patrick Marber
Martin McDonagh
Alistair McDowall
Arthur Miller
Tom Murphy
Phyllis Nagy
Anthony Neilson
Peter Nichols
Ben Okri
Joe Orton
Vinay Patel
Joe Penhall
Luigi Pirandello
Stephen Poliakoff
Lucy Prebble
Peter Quilter
Mark Ravenhill
Philip Ridley
Willy Russell
Sam Shepard
Martin Sherman
Chris Shinn
Jackie Sibblies Drury
Wole Soyinka
Simon Stephens
Kae Tempest
Laura Wade
Anne Washburn
Timberlake Wertenbaker
Roy Williams
Snoo Wilson
Theatre Workshop
Frances Ya-Chu Cowhig
Benjamin Zephaniah

Methuen Drama Student Editions

Alan Ayckbourn *Confusions* • **Mike Bartlett** *Earthquakes in London* • **Aphra Behn** *The Rover* • **Alice Birch** *Revolt. She Said. Revolt Again* • **Edward Bond** *Lear* • *Saved* • **Bertolt Brecht** *The Caucasian Chalk Circle* • *Fear and Misery in the Third Reich* • *The Good Person of Szechwan* • *Life of Galileo* • *Mother Courage and her Children* • *The Resistible Rise of Arturo Ui* • *The Threepenny Opera* • **Jon Brittain** *Rotterdam* • **Georg Büchner** *Woyzeck* • **Anton Chekhov** *The Cherry Orchard* • *The Seagull* • *Three Sisters* • *Uncle Vanya* • **Caryl Churchill** *Serious Money* • *Top Girls* • **Shelagh Delaney** *A Taste of Honey* • **Inua Ellams** *Barber Shop Chronicles* • **Euripides** *Elektra* • *Medea* • **Dario Fo** *Accidental Death of an Anarchist* • **Michael Frayn** *Copenhagen* • **John Galsworthy** *Strife* • **Nikolai Gogol** *The Government Inspector* • **Carlo Goldoni** *A Servant to Two Masters* • **James Graham** *This House* • **Tanika Gupta** *The Empress* • **Katori Hall** *The Mountaintop* • **Lorraine Hansberry** *A Raisin in the Sun* • **Robert Holman** *Across Oka* • **Henrik Ibsen** *A Doll's House* • *Ghosts* • *Hedda Gabler* • **Sarah Kane** *4.48 Psychosis* • *Blasted* • **Charlotte Keatley** *My Mother Said I Never Should* • **Dennis Kelly** *DNA* • **Bernard Kops** *Dreams of Anne Frank* • **Federico García Lorca** *Blood Wedding* • *Doña Rosita the Spinster* (bilingual edition) • *The House of Bernarda Alba* (bilingual edition) • *Yerma* (bilingual edition) • **David Mamet** *Glengarry Glen Ross* • *Oleanna* • **Patrick Marber** *Closer* • **John Marston** *The Malcontent* • **Martin McDonagh** *The Lieutenant of Inishmore* • *The Lonesome West* • *The Beauty Queen of Leenane* • *The Cripple of Inishmaan* • **Alistair McDowall** *Pomona* • **John McGrath** *The Cheviot, the Stag and the Black, Black Oil* • **Arthur Miller** *All My Sons* • *The Crucible* • *A View from the Bridge* • *Death of a Salesman* • *The Price* • *After the Fall* • *The Last Yankee* • *A Memory of Two Mondays* • *Broken Glass* • *Incident at Vichy* • *The American Clock* • *The Ride Down Mt. Morgan* • **Joe Orton** *Loot* • **Joe Penhall** *Blue/Orange* • **Luigi Pirandello** *Six Characters in Search of an Author* • **Lucy Prebble** *Enron* • **Mark Ravenhill** *Shopping and F***ing* • **Reginald Rose** *Twelve Angry Men* • **Willy Russell** *Blood Brothers* • *Educating Rita* • **Lemn Sissay** Benjamin Zephaniah's *Refugee Boy* • **Sophocles** *Antigone* • *Oedipus the King* • **Wole Soyinka** *Death and the King's Horseman* • **Simon Stephens** *Punk Rock* • *Pornography* • **Shelagh Stephenson** *The Memory of Water* • **August Strindberg** *Miss Julie* • **J. M. Synge** *The Playboy of the Western World* • **Kae Tempest** *Wasted* • **Theatre Workshop** *Oh What a Lovely War* • **Laura Wade** *Posh* • **Frank Wedekind** *Spring Awakening* • **Timberlake Wertenbaker** *Our Country's Good* • **Arnold Wesker** *The Merchant* • **Peter Whelan** *The Accrington Pals* • **Oscar Wilde** *The Importance of Being Earnest* • **Roy Williams** *Sing Yer Heart Out for the Lads* • **Tennessee Williams** *A Streetcar Named Desire* • *The Glass Menagerie* • *Cat on a Hot Tin Roof* • *Sweet Bird of Youth*